Killers, Lovers, and Saints

Killers, Lovers, and Saints

ENZO MONTEIRO

RESOURCE *Publications* · Eugene, Oregon

KILLERS, LOVERS, AND SAINTS

Copyright © 2024 Enzo Monteiro. All rights reserved. Except for brief quotations in critical publications or reviews, no part of this book may be reproduced in any manner without prior written permission from the publisher. Write: Permissions, Wipf and Stock Publishers, 199 W. 8th Ave., Suite 3, Eugene, OR 97401.

Resource Publications
An Imprint of Wipf and Stock Publishers
199 W. 8th Ave., Suite 3
Eugene, OR 97401

www.wipfandstock.com

PAPERBACK ISBN: 979-8-3852-1609-3
HARDCOVER ISBN: 979-8-3852-1610-9
EBOOK ISBN: 979-8-3852-1611-6

04/29/24

Contents

PART I | KILLERS

As You Wait for the Flood	3
The Man with a Cross on His Hand	5
Letter to the Feathered Girl	9
Bloodstains and Smoke (Piano Song)	15
Moonlight for the Stables	20
Aboard the Phantom Train	25
Feline, Made of Shadows	29
Don't Cheat the Hangman	35
Why Follow the Wake?	40
Never Murder an Angel	44

PART II | LOVERS

For Death Is My Lover	51
Pictures of Ashes in the Barn	53
The Truth about the Snake	60
Postcard from the Seven Hills	65
Let the Strings Fly (Macramé)	72
The Bride, the Dancer, and the Fox	76
I Picked a Lily	81

The Book in the Park	86
How to Paint a Delicate One	90
A Prayer for the One	95

PART III | SAINTS

I'll Turn the World's Pain into Ink	103
Creation	107
Birth of the Almighty	110
The Word, in the Lord's Bird	114
Escaping the Devil's Tavern	117
Conquering Hell on White, Wild Horses	123
Salvation under Northern Lights	127
Don't Let Me Die on this Mountain	133
Gather Them All for Salvation	138
I'm Getting Married	142

PART I

Killers

AS YOU WAIT FOR THE FLOOD

There's a melody to suffering
That only the smallest birds know
While the featherless burn, clamoring
That what kills you is what you sow

They gather in the emptiest of choirs
Sing of sin and fire in hollow tongues
While their wrinkled fingers paint the desires
That slowly perish in forgotten songs

The voices are anchored by pieces of the moon
They dip and fall so far below its hue
That it makes those with carved skins swoon
And chant that you can learn to love them too

Rest assured that the sun does get weary
Of shining upon the weak and dreary
Those whose only offering is their rage
Confessing to the snake in their cage

My patience has grown as thin as the hairs
On those scalps that you collect in your prayers
Make sure that there is no poison in your blood
You'll need to run or wait for the flood

Gather your clothes and your wives
Wonder if you'll be the one who survives
Don't wave at the black-laden widows
As they kneel in their golden meadows

Amidst the screams and that one whisper
All you'll keep is your bottle of liquor
It's all written in this yellow-paged book
The one at which you're too afraid to look

For you know the truth, it's all over your mirror
Behind your eyes that you've beaten red
From all these incantations that you've read
Tell me, in which one did you find a savior?

When the nations break and turn into clans
Staining lives with the work of their hands
It will take you more than a kiss from your blades
To escape, as the memory of your name fades

It isn't a war if no one is left
After the pillaging, blaspheming and theft
I have many names, you can call me Death
Or confess that I am God with one last breath.

THE MAN WITH A CROSS ON HIS HAND

There is a man, somewhere
With a cross etched on his hand
And he only wears black

He seems as tall as the trees
His voice, low as their roots
His eyes, rarely to be seen
Behind all the smoke

He is only to be found at night
In certain places
Where the potions are poured
Those that make you forget

Be mindful of how you address him
He doesn't like being interrupted
As he's trying to feel
If poison has any effect on him

Go to him, and tell him clearly
Where your pain is
And that you want
To make it go away

He won't look at you
He won't say a word
But he'll pour you one

Then another
And another
A few more after that
And another

He'll leave, and you'll know
That you're supposed
To follow him

He'll take you to a graveyard
You'll stand as still
As a drunkard can be
And he'll finally speak

"Look at that tombstone
And dare telling me
That people understand
Life and death

The man buried there
Is standing before you
It's my name that you could have read
I erased it a long time ago

The liquids had taken their toll
And my pulse was too afraid
Of me waking up
It just stopped

They buried me
Even further underground
Than the saying goes

I awoke surrounded by wood
And I knew what had happened
Fitting end for one
Who always wanted to leave
But never wanted to go away

I dug through the oak
With nothing but my fingernails
They're gone, now
I rose again, like some decaying prophet

No mere man-made box
Can keep me down
But this life, out in the cold air
That's the biggest trap of all

I'm bound to this cursed haze
Amidst the shattered glass
From the broken flasks

Is that what you seek?
An existence with a hand
Constantly reaching for the barrels?

You've seen all these men
Closing their teary eyes
Gulping the sorrows down
Do you think that's

Ever going to take them anywhere?
They're as immobile and swollen
As ugly paintings in abandoned attics

You say that your heart is dead
Then rip it out of your chest
And scream at it
To start beating again

The truth is only found
In what you make it to be
Tell yourself
That you'll see daylight again

Don't seek lovers
Not for a while
And realize
That they're never worth
Dying for

Now leave me be
I must go
I have a woman to find
I'll let her kill me
For good

I've had enough
I'm tired.
I just want to sleep
For good, this time."

LETTER TO THE FEATHERED GIRL

"Loving stranger,
I hope that this letter
Finds you well

I know that it's only been
A short night since
I had to ride away
From you

But your delicate face
Is all that's on my mind
I'm writing to you
Everything that I didn't
Have the time to say

The night that we spent
Seeing each other fleetingly
Will never leave me

Who would have thought
That one of my drunken meanderings
Through this dull and dry prairie
Would lead me to such tender arms

I found you on the side of the trail
Sitting and singing
Next to a dim campfire

I didn't know your language
But you knew mine
You didn't hear me, at first
Or you pretended not to

I don't blame you
For who wants to address
A drunkard after midnight?

I threw my bottle to the ground
Mumbled something
That was insulting
And was about to leave

That's when you told me to wait
There was something in my voice
That was worrying you

And I fell off my horse

I managed to stumble to you
You put your hands on my cheeks
I leaned in for a kiss
And you slapped me harder
Than my mother ever did

You wanted to take
A good look at my eyes
You told me that they were sheltering
Some deep longing and pain

I dismissed it, of course
I wanted to change the subject
I mentioned the feathers
That you use as a hairpin

I asked you where you were from
You told me
About your tribe
And how you had just fled

That you were tired
Of the endless fighting
Between your people and mine

That you were always one
To talk to the spirits
Living through every part of nature

That you were frowned upon
For you wanted to follow them
Guided by the wind

You always felt bridled
Between the tents and the bison
With their bitter meat

Your brethren didn't want to hear
About your wishing
Upon an escapade, anymore

You were told that your place
Was in the elders' shadows
And in silence, always

That very night
You stole your father's horse
And galloped away
As far as you could

That's where you met me
My steed, and my empty whiskey bottle
I presume that I was also
Running away from something

It might be the emptiness
That I always feel
In this so-called civilized world

It's only gunfights and debauchery
Grave-digging out of greed
Empty churches and full gallows

And as I was fighting back
Those rare tears of mine
You kissed me

The hours we spent as one
Made me feel as alive
As I'd ever been

But I heard the distant galloping
It couldn't have been anything good
At that time of night
Between a hill and a coyote's skull

We heard the tribal chants
And you gasped
They'd found you
They were taking you back

You put your hand on mine
As I was drawing my gun
Telling me to run away

That you couldn't be seen
Lost in passion with a white man
Especially not after fleeing from home
And bringing disgrace to your peers

I jumped on my horse
And managed to ride away
As shots were being fired

I'm now writing to you
From my small town
My back against the church wall
A few feet away from the makeshift graves

How convenient, my sweet
For you didn't see it
But a bullet reached my side
I'm bleeding out rapidly

I want you to know all of it
But I don't know how this letter
Will ever find you

For I now realize
That you never
Told me your name.

BLOODSTAINS AND SMOKE (PIANO SONG)

This garment of black
That you've sowed for me
Is now drenched in red

I sit on this broken bed
Look at your side of it
And you're not there

This house is now only
Shattered glass under
My naked feet

I don't care about
Those cuts anymore
I've already felt
The worst one of all

I walk around
The garden at night
And leave a trail of red
On the fresh grass

I've been made aimless
By this one evening
This piece of lightning
That I never heard

I don't want to wake up
Without you by my side
But I'm so numb that I can't
Even find the strength
To kill myself

I roam this house
That we once called ours
I look at the pictures
And rip the halves that I'm on

It's only you, it's always been
I don't want to see anything else
I've been drawing your face
On every surface

Now you're all around
As if you'd never left
But it still fails to bring
A smile to my face

I take every cigarette
That I find in these old drawers
And I start to smoke them all

I'll light them up
Until the fire runs out
In this room
And in my mind

Make me choke
Make me drown
In this gray cloud
That I try to hide in

May it all be set ablaze
Consume me, make me feel
Something else than the emptiness
That you've left me with

I don't know what else I should do
Except go to this piano of ours
That you always said was too out of tune
For any pretty song to come from it

Allow me to sit there
And see if the keys
Can feel the pain
Of my bloody fingers

But first, let me put
This knife on top of it
It'll inspire me

I look at it and the notes
Show themselves
Resigned and low
Wary of me

The words come to me
And I sing softly

"Pour the wine
All around me
Light a match
And see if it's enough
To make me catch fire

Keep just enough of it
To make yourself a drink
And have a haze
To lose yourself in

Hold me tightly
As we let the flames
Remind us of what our love
Always felt like

Kiss me tenderly
Look at me in the eyes
Promise me that
I'll see you
On the other side

Sign your name
On the Pearly Gates
For me to know
That you got there safely

I'll be right with you."

I stop playing
It's getting late
I must go to sleep

But first, I must remove
Your dead body
From the bedroom floor
And throw the knife away.

MOONLIGHT FOR THE STABLES

"Sweet one, it's about time
That you leave this place
It makes you ache
It makes you cry

The sun doesn't forgive
Those who don't seek
The shade's soft release

Here you stand
From its rising
To its setting
But for what?

Those horses that you take
Such loving care of
Don't you think
That they'd be happier
If you set them free?

You're just like them
You've been bridled
A pretty thing on display
Cursed to running in circles

The moon is high, tonight
It shines so brightly
Your room is bathing in it
And you can't sleep

You look at the horses
From your window
Sleeping up straight
Dreaming of lying down

I've always told you
That I'd be waiting for you
In front of the ballroom
Where we met

I'm there every night
But I know that you won't come
Unless something catches fire
Either the stables, or your mind

Tonight, I caved in
I found the small, broken mirror
That you gifted me as a souvenir
When we both fell in the river

I'm letting the moonlight
Bounce off it
Straight into your room

I'd play you a song
For you to come down
But we can't afford
To wake your parents up

They never liked me
To them, I've always been
A lowlife, a drifter
Stuck in his blues

I finally see your delicate figure
So pure, in your white gown
You smile, and come down

We kiss, for the first time
In many a tiring day
And a mournful night

Without saying a word
I take your hand
And guide you

I tell you to close your eyes
I have a surprise for you
You must trust me

I let you open them
And your mouth opens wide
When you see
What I came to give you

Two beautiful steeds
That will lead us
Straight to freedom

I won them playing cards
I didn't want to steal anything
From your family
And their livelihood

You embrace me tightly
We get on our saddles
I'm ready to go

You're looking at your house
It's tough to leave behind, I know
Remember that it has brought you nothing
But a pain that shouldn't be felt
When we're this young and wild

We start riding out
We have a whole life
To build together

And who knows,
Maybe one day
I'll find the courage
To tell you

That after that game of cards
Where I won the horses fairly
　　The man got mad
　　A fight ensued

　　And I killed him."

ABOARD THE PHANTOM TRAIN

I'm riding a train
That is only
To be seen at night

No one speaks, here
But I can hear sobbing
Between the old drunks
And the women dressed in black

I feel like an impostor
Those people
Or what's left of them
Seem to know a pain
That I can't imagine

There's an old man
Sitting across from me
He hasn't stopped looking
At the picture in his hand

He catches me looking
He grins at me
And it's the saddest smile
That I've ever seen

He shows the picture to me
Him, a woman
Two children
In front of a big house

He tells me

"See, young man
Where the vines grow
Is where I'm not
To be found again

My haven, the place
That I'd promised
To make sense of

It's been overtaken
By time, after it got
Rid of me and my strength
And by tears, as they formed
Stains on the floorboards

I'd been given
A saint and two angels
To protect

I failed.

Oh, young man
How I failed.

I couldn't crawl my way out
Of the grip that the bottles
Had over my dreams and I

They were all
Backwards words
Cracked walls
And broken stained glass

I lost all my money
My home was shaped
By shivers and cries
From sorrow and hunger

I couldn't accept it
I drank some more
Until I forgot
My own name

I fell asleep on a boat
That took me to hell
And then back

I don't know how long
I roamed around the streets for
Making anyone avoid
The town drunk

When I finally remembered
That I existed, that I could breathe
I came back to the house
The trees had claimed it back

Not a sound inside
Not my delicate wife
Or my joyful sons

Only this picture
That wasn't ripped
But I am

Even if I found them
I couldn't talk to them
For you see, young man
I did cease to breathe and exist
I made sure of that

We're all dead on this train."

FELINE, MADE OF SHADOWS

Feline, made of shadows
Do you wait for the night
To share your colors
For you to roam the streets?

I can only see your green eyes
Shining like sunbathing emeralds
But I'm stumbling on the pavement
As the blood runs down my face

Let me ask you, perpetual bad sign
Has my luck run out yet?
It certainly feels that way

May I sit here?
You can keep your distance
I know that you are
A wary creature

It's been a long day
As you can see
My face isn't usually
Drenched in red

You look at me
With such curiosity
I've seen it before

There used to be woman
Who, just like you
Would look at me
From afar

She didn't know what to make
Of the heaviness that she perceived
In my eyes, always

And when she sensed
That I wasn't one
To hurt any living thing
She got closer

She didn't say much
Just like you, she was more
Of the staring kind

We spent every night
From that point on
With our shoulder
Against the other's

There was something in the stars
We were both
Trying to spell out

I'm still doing it
With her name
Though she never told me
What it was

We walked along the river
Underneath this huge bridge
That makes me dizzy
Every time I look up at it

She said that we should
Climb all the steps
That lead to its top

For us to finally see the city
The way it's meant to be painted
As we finally free ourselves
Of the ground beneath our feet

We reached the top
I was out of breath
But she was so agile
She moved with such grace

And before I could reach her
To gaze at all those lights
That were making her cry
She looked at me in terror

I felt a hand on my shoulder
I turned around, and I saw
A man, with the purest anger
In the way he was looking at me

He hit me so hard
That I barely remember it
I dropped to the ground
And he kept beating me

She ran to him
Trying to pull him off
In the haze, I heard
That they used to be lovers

He grabbed me by the neck
Took me to the edge of the bridge
He was ready to throw me off it

As he pushed me
She grabbed my arm
Trying to catch me
She ended up falling
Instead of me

I'd never seen anything
Happen so slowly
Time might as well
Have stopped

For the sight to hurt even more
He looked at me in horror
His demeanor had changed
He was trying to make amends

But the numbness had set
Too deeply at my core
For me to even consider
Forgiveness

I pushed him off too

Now I realize
That they're together
In death

But isn't it better
Than being alone
In life?

Thank you for listening
You're still keeping your distance
It's better this way
You know what happens
To whomever gets close.

DON'T CHEAT THE HANGMAN

"As you stand in this prairie
You find yourself
Drenched in red
Wondering what happened

Your clothes are torn
You're out of breath
You're lying against the only tree
That's to be found for miles

Your satchel is next to you
Your horse must have died
As you were fleeing
From whomever
Was trying to hurt you

It's only as the sun rises
That you come to your senses
But what good are they
If you're covered with bruises?

Your eyes are swollen
Your ears are ringing
Your hands are as good as broken
And you keep spitting blood

You must find a clue
Somewhere, to help you
Understand what happened

Search your pockets
And you'll find a torn picture
Of a beautiful woman

Hair of wheat, eyes of emerald
But you can't even remember
Your own name, let alone hers

Where will you go now?
Crying won't help you
Bring the memories back
And the tears will only burn
The wounds on your face

As you give in to despair
A wild dog comes to you
He looks friendly

He lies down next to you
As a faithful companion
For you to share your pain with

There is a bottle of cheap whiskey
Somewhere in your satchel
Grab it, drink from it
And forget some more

Walk for hours on end
With your new friend
Under the blistering heat

Go on, start drinking
Start walking
Stop living

Wait, that taste
It's bringing it back
To you, slowly
It flashes quickly

The woman, in your arms
A house that you built
A child ready to be born

A long night at the saloon
A game of cards
A sore loser, his face punched in
And violent threats made

You walked home one day
And you found your home
Burned to a crisp

With your beloved woman outside
Lying on her side, in the dirt
With two bullets in her back

The flames overtook your mind
And you waited there
For the whole night
You knew that they'd come back

You prayed to the Lord
That he'd make you
An instrument of death
To exact revenge
On the worst of sinners

You had a dream
Where one of his angels
Came to you, and told you
That their time would come

That you should pray for healing
Rather than for murder
And that the Lord
Would strike them down himself

Reminding you that,
In the land of flesh and bones
You're still under the law of man
And that no one cheats the hangman

But you didn't listen
You couldn't hear anything
Your heart was beating
Too loudly

You finally heard horses
Galloping in the distance
Getting closer and closer

Four men arrived and laughed
Seeing you standing there
With only a six shooter and a knife

What exactly happened
You still don't remember
But there you were, standing over
Their dead bodies

That's when you got on your horse
And rode so far, so fast
That your steed collapsed

Now you can see a cloud of dust
In the distance, in that prairie
Where one could watch his dog
Run away for days

Tell your own dog to do so

It must be the town folks
Looking for the man
Who murdered four others
And who are very quick
To lead one to the gallows

Start walking towards them
You know the price you'll have to pay
Revenge is a fool's game
God himself told you."

WHY FOLLOW THE WAKE?

I wear black
In mourning
Of this life
That I can't attain

I'm part of a wake
That has always existed
And that will never cease

I don't know
Whose funeral it is
That I'm attending

I'm the only one
Who ever stops
To take a breath
And look around

The others are hiding their eyes
Behind impenetrable shades
Well, so am I
But I wear them everywhere else

There's a fire burning somewhere
I can feel its distant warmth
And taste the smoke

There's a forest to the west
The green leaves are so
Dark and thick
That no light comes through

I've always wondered
What's to be found
Between its branches

Maybe this time
I'll diverge from the procession
And try to explore it
No one has ever looked at me
They wouldn't notice my absence

I get off the beaten path
Reach the forest
And walk among the trees

It's so dark on this sunny day
Not a single noise
No cracking of the leaves
No humming of the birds

I rest my hand on a trunk
And I can feel
A thick liquid
On my hand

I can barely see
I have to taste it
It's blood
I can feel the rust in the air

I'm letting it guide me
To another tree
With another fresh stain
I keep following it

The pools of red
Get more frequent
Until I find a trail

It takes me to a clearing
Where light is finally
To be found

There is a body lying there
Face down on the damp grass
I must go help
I turn it over

My heart stops
It's me
That I'm facing

My body
My white garment
Drenched in red

I was shot
I crawled
All the way to the clearing
To get some peace, maybe

Under the sun
The light that I knew
To follow

Those people
That I was following
Were carrying my body
In that box

NEVER MURDER AN ANGEL

The fallen angel
Rests among us
Lying on the grass
That he drenched with red

Two bullet wounds
But who could have killed
Such a pure, holy being?

A choir's chants
Resonate from above
As if the skies
Were opening wide

God himself
Shows his face
Some of us
Can't take it

Many fall dead
Crushed by the sight
Of the mightiest one

He's sitting on the throne
Surrounded by thousands of angels
Who mourn their fallen brother

In their weeping, they still sound
More beautiful than the purest voices
And the most delicate instruments
That man has ever made

Only a few of us remain standing
Ready to be struck
And never meeting him again

But he comes down to us
And closes the clouds
Behind him

He speaks

"My children,
What have you done?
I had sent you a most beloved one
To help you through your pain

One who wasn't subject to sin
Who can sew garments
Out of the most immaculate
Shade of white

To be a confidant to the friendless
To be a messenger to the mute
To be a guide to the blind
To be a dancer to the deaf

How is it
That you show
Your gratitude
To him and to me?

Your wickedness has led you
To killing a piece of heaven
What should I make of you
And your murderous intent?

I wanted to give you all wings
He was going to take you
Back with him
If only you'd let him

Yet here he lays
In a sacrifice
That I never wanted
Which one of you would be ready
To go through what he did?

I thought that this world
Was going to learn
From its brokenness

That I am the place
For you to call home
That my embrace
Gives life to everything

But you were poisoned
Far too long ago
You got accustomed
To the blackness of your veins

Do you ever see
Any color around you
Except the red
Of the blood that you spill?

If this is all a canvas
For you to paint
Your suffering on
Then will you burn it?

I'd take the fire away from you
I'd rebuke you all
Even the women and children

You would kneel
You would beg
You would submit

But I love you, my children
I don't want you to suffer
Despite what you did

I have made a mistake
By letting you roam around
After the first time
You ever lied to me

The sin is flowing too deeply
It's a muddy river that you all
Keep drinking from

You could have been one with me
You could have sung my praise
You could have been eternally blessed

Yet you chose silence
You chose darkness
You chose death."

God sheds a tear
He lifts his arms
The earth shatters
The clouds roar with lightning

Before we can feel any pain
It all fades to black.

PART II

Lovers

FOR DEATH IS MY LOVER

I'm in a valley
Standing, breathing
How could it be?

I remember the crash
Screams, pieces of broken glass
The smell of fire

There she comes
Long white dress
Black cloak
She removes the hood

She's beautiful
Dark hair and eyes
Peaceful smile
Enticing

She invites me to sit
There's a chessboard
We play in the grass
I can't help but look at her

"Checkmate," I say
"You win. You must go back," she replies

I don't want to
I want to stay by her side
She appeases me

I try to touch her hand
The earth swallows me whole

I emerge from the smoking, crushed car
Bloody and bruised, but alive
I know she's out there, somewhere.

PICTURES OF ASHES IN THE BARN

I see that burnt down barn
Under a colorless moon
The one that I usually keep
In the last drawer
Of my bedside table

I can't help but to enter it
To try to understand
What or who used to live there
And if there's anything left

I already know
The answer is a foregone conclusion
But I must see it
With my own eyes

Surely enough, it's filled
With half burnt pictures
And all that remains
Is my face, unscathed

Whoever it was
That set them ablaze
Wanted to keep the image
Of me alive
But not theirs, not by my side

I gather them all
But I have no way of knowing
Who it is that I've hurt
So badly

It could be many different women
I've been a careless lover
Between the bottomless bottles
And the pistol-shaped poetry
About salvation and death

I must find a clue
Before other pieces
Of our shared memory
Are reduced to ashes

Some small bits
Of bright yellow
Are scattered on the floor

I look closer, and I realize
That they're the petals
Of a once bright sunflower

The color is faded
Like the ill-fated promise
Of love I must have given

I collect the small, frail reminders
That flowers catch fire
Faster than paper
Yet they survived

I'm ready to give up
I sit with my back
Against what remains
Of the entrance wall

And that's when I see it
So huge, so obvious
It makes my heart burst

On the opposite wall
Drawn so wide and desperately
With uneven lines
As if by a shaking hand

This star, which was meant
To guide me to a life
Of all the safety
That sincere love provides

The one etched on the chest
Of my most devoted sweetheart
The one who would have never
Given up on me

But I did, so abruptly
Despite all my pretty words
My nocturnal declarations
Of a passion that wasn't given
Enough light to fully blossom

In the middle of it
I can see a shelf
That was left untouched
In the midst
Of the broken-hearted flames

On it, I find a letter
That I'm afraid to open
But I do nonetheless
She deserves to be heard and read

It says

"Beloved stranger,
Whom I thought I knew
Please find these words

Not of resentment
But deep sorrow
Over what could have been

I was ready to give it
All up for you
My silly dreams
Away from your embrace

I would have given you
The most beautiful of children
And taken care of you
Through your darkest dreams

If it's only the lust
That was eating away at you
Then I would have accepted
To save myself, until we became one

All you needed to do
Was to say the word
I would have done anything
For you

I would have collected
Every drop of rain
Falling from the leaves
Of this forest we liked
To get lost in

I would have put them all
In small jars, dispersed them
Around the world
For you never to be afraid
Of drowning again

For every song and poem
That you wrote for me
I would have written
Two more of, for you
In secret

And when we finally
Would have become one flesh
Under God's protection
I would have given you the book
Made of all those words

I was ready to give my life
To the savior, that you always
Were afraid of disappointing

But now I sit here, alone
Wondering why God sent me
Such an enticing man
Only to take him away from me

I've been finding refuge
In this barn, when I can't sleep
Ever since you left me
To gaze at the stars by myself

I want to leave it behind, now
I must make it disappear
And start anew

But I find myself hoping
That some pieces of it
Will survive the ignition
For you to remember me

If this letter survives
Keep it with you
In your back pocket, always
Until the ink fades
If it ever does.

THE TRUTH ABOUT THE SNAKE

You came along
I couldn't see
A piece of me hit you
Inadvertently

You asked for my name
I didn't try to hide
You liked my honesty

I couldn't have known
That you'd been onto me
Since the beginning

The little cabin
In the back of the garden
Looked like a small world
That could have hosted us both
And no one else

They all fell asleep
But not us
It wasn't to be denied
This pulsating need
To get closer

For the smiling hadn't ceased
Not once
We got locked in a room
By one who thought
That he was helping us

He facilitated my demise
But I didn't know
How was I supposed to?

The world didn't seem
To hold anything else
Than what it was showing
On the surface
Not then, at least

You couldn't push me
Off the bed
So you said
That there was room for two

You lay there
I came up
With a stupid line
That somehow worked

We kissed
It was nice and warm
I told you
You said that you knew

Did you bite me
When I was asleep?
I don't remember
Any immediate pain

But for the following weeks
I could feel it, I was becoming
A stranger to myself
Slowly, surely

Is this the metaphor
Or is it me telling the tale?
You started it all

You're the reason
So many words
Have been written
On my dirty pages

You lingered on
And still do, sometimes
For me to avoid the pain
I let the idea of me be poisoned

This isn't another part of the fable
I just had never taken the time
To make it barebones
And describe it as it was

There will still be fevers
I like to give colors to shadows
And try to hold their hands
You always hated that in me

Yet you were the one
Complaining about
My lack of joy

But, lost one,
You have the saddest eyes
That I've ever seen

Where are they now?
What are you looking at?
Not me, I'm gone
You made sure of that

I don't resent you
I did, for a long time
The pull was as strong
As it was stillborn

I saw you twice more
It made my heart burst
At least I knew
That I was still alive

You led to it all
The toxins too
But it made me forget
Everything for you

In a way, you'll always be here
You're the snake
You're the poison
You're the foregone conclusion.

POSTCARD FROM THE SEVEN HILLS

"Hey there,
It's me again
I know that we just
Saw each other yesterday

I want you to know
That I had a wonderful time
Walking these hills
That you love so much

So many viewpoints
You showed me
And yet the only thing I saw
Was you

I was trying to get lost
And then found in your eyes
But it took you a while
To let me see them

I understand, it's not easy
To let a stranger
Get so close to you

But you're the one
Who asked me
To take the trip down south
Only you know why

It doesn't really matter
I'm glad that I made it
And that we spent half a day
In the same world

Your timid laughter
Your blushing when your friend
Told me that I could find
A lover in you

Those are the things
That I'm taking home with me
A place where these moments
Of unborn romance
Only happen in my mind

When the sun was up
Blinding me, preventing me
From taking your sight in
I could feel the empty space
That you created between us

I wish I could have
Stayed by your side more
But I, too, have people with me
Trying to protect the only
Heartstrings that remain

When I asked you
If we could all sit down
It was only for time
To take a rest
And join us at the table

That's when daylight
Started giving way
To a colder evening breeze

You used the potions
To warm yourself up
I don't know if you cared
About how it pained me
To look at them

You said that you needed them
To speak one of my languages
But you barely ever did

You talked about how
I'm one to break into song
Whenever I'm trying
To ignite a fire

I wish I'd taken
My poor man's harp with me
To show you exactly
What it's about

But I'd made a promise
Not to make my bed
Out of warm ashes
Anymore

I tried to make
My lips and fingers
As cold as I could
For you to be afraid
Of their touch

Fleeting, tiny collisions
Those I tend to find
Too much meaning in
I couldn't avoid them

I was still doing well
Avoiding the piercing glare
Of one who's out to protect me
From myself

But our journey wasn't over
There was one last place
That you wanted to show me

We walked up some more
As the sky was finally
Shedding off its golden shades

That's where I saw it
What you'd been telling me
About the view
Of this city that you cherish

I tried to take it all in
The peaceful river, wide as a sea
And the distant cars
Traveling to where life is found

But the image couldn't
Leave an imprint on my mind
For you were already there

I allowed myself
A single moment
Of weak reprieve
And walked to you

I asked your friend
To leave us
If only for a little while

You almost asked him
Not to leave you alone with me
But I presume, and hope
That you gave in
To the picturesque moment, too

That's when I finally caught them
Your hazel eyes, for myself only
I realized that I never wanted
To look at anything else again

There were so many things
That I know we both wanted
To talk about, but didn't
Out of fear of uncertainty

But that moment,
That one piece of warm wind
Blowing through us
I wish it had never stopped

Surrounded by the city lights
And everything that you wanted me
To know about your world
We made it only about you and me

You broke it off,
But I understand
It had to end
At least for a while

I'd rather let the candle
Burn slowly and gently
Than dance with you
In a wild bonfire

We walked down
And I feel like I still am
Will you come back to me
When I end up in the river?

Someday, hopefully soon
I'll be able to show you
The town that adopted me
Though I didn't want
Anything to do with it, at first

A dream,
Or a premonition
I don't know yet
I don't think I want to

No matter what happens
The moment that we shared
Will never be erased

I'll keep reliving it
No matter how much it hurts
That it had to end

Sincerely,

Your favorite stranger."

LET THE STRINGS FLY (MACRAMÉ)

This owl that I saw
On a rooftop
In broad daylight
Will you make something out of it?

You take the strings
And give them life
It's quite endearing

Can you write a play?
I'm sure you could create
Some lovely characters
And let them be happy

They wouldn't have to talk
So colorful they'd be
That their pigments
Would reveal it all

Now I wonder how long
Their limbs would be
If it makes you so enthralled
That you never stop?

Stretching it out
Trying to make them smile
How much fabric does it take
To create some peace?

You have the secret of creation
Right at your fingertips
I'd ask you to teach me
But I wouldn't feel worthy

I'm one for the words
You're one for all
That takes shape
And is beautifully displayed

On the walls
Next to the paintings
For the chosen few to see
And marvel at

Hang it above your bed
Chase the bad dreams away
It's as if
You were casting spells

Nothing will remain hollow
When you're around
You'll take good care
Of your little creations

I'll look at them
If you let me
I'll smile and wonder
Where I can find
Such dexterity

For if I can't give life to myself
Maybe I can relish
In the fables that come to me
When my mind wanders

Keep going
Make it true
Make people see
Only if they deserve it

It's pure and anew
It's watched upon
By some winged beings
Blessing you with their softness

Don't leave them out in the rain
Keep them close to the warmth
That you feel
When you stitch them together

A fireplace, a reflection in the pupils
Of those who are willing to stop
And look around a bit more
For the appeasing details

Like the bird that I saw
And the life that you seek
It's in the little things
Keep looking

If the strings fly around
Let them be
They won't harm anyone
You can start over

The flow isn't interrupted
It just changes
It's ripples on a lake
It's a current in the air

Trust your senses
And your hands
You're creating
Your own company

Small friends, tiny landscapes
They'll stay with you
If you trust yourself
In making them

A feather near you
One that you won't see
But I do
I'll encourage you

THE BRIDE, THE DANCER, AND THE FOX

Walking down this aisle
That I thought
Had burnt down

In a church, the kind
That's illuminated
By grandiose stained glass

She comes to me, slowly
In her white gown
Doing her perfect smile
A thousand favors

Her hair is tied
Its fire is tamed
Like a China doll princess
Sheltering an oasis sun

The choir sings
It reverberates
I can't see anyone else
It's only her

Candles showing the way
We're so close
I'm almost complete

We finally face each other
We're both trying to contain
The fireflies in our chests

And as the holy words are spoken
We lose ourselves
In each other's pupils

We're found in all the times
When loving was so easy
Away from anything worldly
Only in godly joy

With her dancing in a field
Bathing in green
As the mist came and went

She wanted to make sure
That I could still find her
Even if my senses failed me

Now in a castle
Those that they build
In the south

Where the lovely dancers
In black and red dresses
Tried to hypnotize
Us hopeless lovers

She was so beautiful
With that rose in her hair
And the red on her lips

With the fan in hand
She blew me away
Ever so gently

With a gesture of her finger
She made me go to her
My body moved by itself
I couldn't resist

With her tender hand
She grabbed the back of my neck
And pulled me so close

All I could hear and feel
Was our breaths
On each other's cheek

Temptation, burning me
From the inside
But we'd made a promise
For it's never too late
To save oneself

Now in that forest
Where she always tried
To find the clearing
Faster every time

We were lying down
Letting God's light
Give us life again

She arose, and told me
That she could hear a stream
One that we'd never noticed before

I couldn't hear it, but I knew better
Than to ever doubt an angel
For they can see it all
As they stand on the clouds

She grabbed my hand
And led me straight
To the purest of streams

We marveled at how peace
Can flow from such
A strong element

In the bushes nearby
She saw a small creature
That she still wishes
She could have called hers

A curious fox, looking at us
From its shaded haven
With eyes so green
That she told me so many times
She wishes she'd had

I'm blinded by a sparkle
And I now realize
That I have the ring in hand
I'm about to make her mine, forever

That's when she dissipates
She must, it's only a vision
But I don't feel sorrow
It was all so clear

It must be a message
There is a parchment, somewhere
That tells this very story
I have to find it

I PICKED A LILY

I was walking
Through a field
By myself

I stumbled upon
An abandoned house
With my name written
On one of the walls

I went inside
What was left of it
By the fallen door
And the broken bell

So many pictures
And paintings hanging
But all the faces
Had been erased

Empty bottles, full ashtrays
Whoever used to live here
Had let themselves go
Along with the house

I made my way
To the other side
Into the garden

Wilted flowers and dead leaves
On the dry grass
What once had been lush green
Was now a pale yellow

I wondered why
My steps had guided me
To such desolation
I was ready to leave

Then it caught my eye
This one pigment
That was refusing to die
I approached it

And I saw it
The only living thing
Around me

A beautiful lily
Of pink and white
Opening itself gently

Suddenly, an apparition
A breath-taking one
Of pale skin and wide smile

I could see through her
She must have been
The gentlest of ghosts

She told me not to be afraid
I could have never been
The sight of her was too pretty
To be driven away by

We sat
As the flower
Kept slowly opening

We talked about God
Salvation and purpose
And why he takes
Our beloved away

She asked me if I thought
That those who die
By their own hand
Still find him

She told me about
Her struggles in trusting him
That she asked him for strength
Every morning

I told her that the decision
Was hers to make
That if she couldn't trust him
She couldn't trust anyone

I told her not to be afraid
For he's always by our side
And that she's infinitely
Worthy to him

She told me to follow
My own advice
She couldn't understand why
I didn't love myself more

We stopped talking
And stared at each other's eyes
I called her beautiful
She called me handsome

I finally found the strength
To ask her why
She was intangible

She told me
That she couldn't be
Real to me
Just yet

But that she might, one day
If I picked the lily
Cherished it, protected it
Gave it sun and water

She faded away
Only for a while
At least I hope

So, I picked the lily

THE BOOK IN THE PARK

A park, with children playing
Birds singing, leaves blowing
We're both lying on the grass
I'm softly playing guitar
While you're reading your favorite book

I ask you if the music
Is distracting you
You reply
That it's making it better

It's allowing you to envision
The characters more clearly
Hear their words
In this passion that wasn't meant to be

I haven't read this one
But you and I aren't on that path
What we have doesn't have any reason
To ever cease

I ask you why they can't be together
You hand me the book
I stop playing
These are the words

"Many nights of bright red
The most enticing of colors
Made us collide, my dear

But I can't get any closer to you
I'm afraid that it's the saddening truth
Of my condition

I am one to pour the toxins
Wherever I roam
To make it all numb
Then set it on fire

It's been years
Maybe even more
it has now
Caught up with me

My body is giving up on me, my love
And how can I give you my heart
If it stops beating?

This trail is of my own design
I'm the only one to blame
And I do, every day

I'm telling you now, my sweet
That it can't, shouldn't be
This isn't the type of passion
That you deserve

Before any more harm is done
And you must make do
With a drunken shell of a man
Whose time is almost up

I retreat, as my only act
Of noble preservation
Of a piece of beauty
That must remain intact

You won't see me anymore
I'm letting the night take me away
Far from you, for no more sadness
To ever come your way

It will hurt at first
And it should
Feel it, cherish it
You're alive
I'm not."

I look at you in distress
And ask who wrote about me
You laugh, and make me lie down
You tell me

"Do you remember when you told me
That dreams can't harm me
Because they'll never be real?

Books are tangible dreams
Those characters are imprisoned
By the will of their writer

It's an irremediable mechanism
That of tragedy's cogwheels
Setting themselves in motion
Towards a bittersweet morale

But you're not in chains
No ink is being used
To dictate your every move

Feel this freedom around
As the sun starts setting
And we find ourselves resting
In this beautiful landscape

You're here, and you're alive
Because you decide to be
What we have is, and will be

The only trail you're leaving behind you
Is one of kindness and devotion
To endlessly amaze me

I'm here, and so are you
The liquids in you
Got diluted, nowhere to be felt anymore
Now, kiss me."

HOW TO PAINT A DELICATE ONE

Delicate one,

Tell me where you went
As you fell asleep
On a bed made
Of those confusing feelings

The fear of leaving home
The joy in finding freedom
The sadness of misplaced love
The mystery of a nocturnal encounter

I wish I could paint them all
Would you let me borrow
The many colors in your eyes
For me to put on my pallet?

I'll build a canvas made of the white
That is found in the feathers
That were abandoned
By those wings you won't show me

I'll start with the sun
For your undying hope
Made from the unwanted golden hue
In your hair once made of wood

I'll take the black
That used to course through my veins
Let it bathe in my newfound joy
To turn it into light blue
And create the skies

I'll ask the Lord for some clay
The purest one, from which he made you
I'll extract its gray shade
To add this hometown of yours
That you refuse to forget

I'll pluck some green
Out of the lie
You keep being told
About your irises

I'll turn it into a meadow
Of such softness
That you'll wish it could
Grab you by the dreams
And never let go

I'll find some pink in your nails
I'll subdue its brightness
I wouldn't want to go blind

I'll use it to add some light clouds
Floating by, showing you
That sunset is near
Ready to greet you with confessions
That are only made at night

But, my dear
Before I let the sun
Sleep on your soft figure
I must add you in

I'll never pretend that my fingers
Can move with enough grace
To imitate the one that I find
In your silhouette

I'll find one of those pictures
That you love to take
When a moment is too beautiful
For you to only remember

One that you refuse
To add to your scrapbook
In which you make sure
That those moments never die

One in which you're shown
In your understated beauty
So much so that you'll refuse
To lay eyes on it, saying
That you don't deserve to be gazed at

It's that very one that I'll use
To finish the painting
For you to finally learn
To look at yourself and smile

Now allow me to bring it to you
During a warm evening where I'll make sure
That the summer breeze makes your hair fly
When you look at me from your window

You'll see me, you'll start speaking
But I won't allow you to ask
Any questions, for we'll need
To remain quiet

We wouldn't want to wake
Any of your friends or neighbors up
They wouldn't understand why
We keep colliding

I'll climb through the window
Tell you to close your eyes
And when you open them
You'll see it hanging
On your wall

We'll both sit on the edge
Of this bed of yours
That's too small
For the two of us

But we needn't worry
About this fire just yet
For we'll both find peace
Looking at it

You'll rest your head on my shoulder
Our breaths will echo each other's
And you'll fall asleep

A PRAYER FOR THE ONE

My Lord, consider this prayer
A written one
For I have a lot to say

I was told to make a list
When wishing to pray
About a special apparition

To make it as vivid
As it could be
Without being real

You know my heart
You know what happened
You set it in motion

I trust your judgment, always
And I'm listening to the words
That you speak through my friends

About slowing down
Standing so perfectly still
That I can almost see
The late autumn breeze

Love isn't a land
For me to roam just yet
It's a recently erupted volcano
With me sitting at the edge of the crater

A single moment of lonely weakness
Could make me fall right back down
To the sinful fire
And the molten pain

Until I'm ready
To gaze upon the world
With rested eyes again
Please hear these words

"I want one whose face
Constantly looks possessed
By youthful wonder

One whose laughter
Is the only sound
That I ever want to hear

One who's ready to walk with me
All the way to the mouth of the beast
To show it to me, let me feel
Its cursed breath, and remind me
That it was never real

One who can pluck the strings
By my side, always
Ready to make her melodies
Intertwine with mine

One who understands the hearts
Of all of those that she sees
On their beaten path
To silent suffering

One who asks the questions
That cut deeply through me
When I don't understand
Why I can't let go of a single tear

One who isn't afraid
Of touching me, holding me
To make sure
That there is still warmth, life
Behind my stern expression

One who tells me
That the pain is to be welcomed
Felt, embraced, spoken to
Until it decides to slip away
All by itself

One who speaks the language
Of the most colorful of hummingbirds
As well as the blackest of crows

One who knows
That there needs to be shade
For the weary travelers to rest in
When the sun is too bright to bear

One who sees the strange shapes in me
And doesn't frown upon them
Instead, turns them into paintings

One who reassures me
When I wonder if I'll ever be
Welcomed back into the highest places."

For, my Lord, finally
And if there were only one wish of mine
She'll be one who fears you, loves you
Is saved by your grace
And your son's sacrifice

She'll know that this life
Isn't our home
That you're waiting for us
Your saints

God almighty
I thank you so much
For being here with me tonight
For listening to me

For bringing me peace and the revelation
Through the Spirit
That she is out there
And that she's looking for me too

PART III
Saints

I'LL TURN THE WORLD'S PAIN INTO INK

Father, you have finally
Brought me clarity
As to where you want
Me to go

I'd been praying for purpose
Worrying over any piece of silence
That was crawling through
The cracks of my day

Wondering if what you wanted
Was for me to grab my guitar
And roam the world
Looking for lonely drifters and women
Waiting for a soft serenade

But the thought didn't bring me peace
And you're only to be found
When the clouds part
And that warm yellow light
Is to be seen

I had almost forgotten about
This vision you had sent my way
During a time that now feels so distant
That I might as well
Not have been born yet

The face of this wordsmith
Poet, singer, man of many muses
Who left such a raw mark
With his turns of phrases alone

That's when I knew that you wanted me
To focus on nothing but spreading
My own treaties on killers, lovers, and saints
To a world that longs for meaning

But life took its toll on me
And those three themes
That I always write about
Became all too real

A few crises of faith
A perpetually broken heart
A will to be my own murderer

I couldn't tell the difference
Between art and life
Only now do I realize
That they're the same

And this morning, you spoke to me
In such a clear and sincere voice
Telling me to forget about the songs
If only for a minute

That the essence of my gift
Has always been the paintings
That I manage to give life to
Merely by spelling them out

That music should only be
To glorify you, and allow the poetry
To sing, twirl, find some romance
Outside of the white pages

You showed me words
That could open gates
To a different kind of kingdom
The fallen one, in need of reprieve
From the hunger, the sin, the death

Father, I now know
That I am just the person
That you have sent
To turn the world's pain into ink

I pray that you give me
Inspiration, always
That my hands never shake
For me to shape the stories
Until they're out of breath

Make sure that my manuscript
Reaches all of those
Who can't find a reason
To keep waking up
And look at the skies

Make them realize
That they're not alone
In the suffering and sense of loss
For I've felt it all many times over

Bring healing through my tales
Of so many unreachable birds
And colorless, wilted flowers

Make me carry the burden
Of a humanity that has forgotten
That you are the only way
To life in its true form

Bestow all these dreary images
Upon my mind and dreams
For me to let them drip
Off everything I say

For all that I touch
To become the diary of everything
That the mute, deaf and blind
Want to scream, hear, and see

Lastly, my Lord
Allow my works
To let them all know about you
For you are where solace is found
I'm only the vessel

CREATION

"I have seen it all

A young girl
Clothed by the moon
Trying to nurse a candle
Into a timid flame

A wounded dog
Leaving a red trail
On the winter soil
For no one to find

An angel refusing
To come back down
For the screams of anguish
Are too painful to hear

A sinner endeavoring
To forget his own name
By making himself sink
From the inside

A widow at the foot
Of her empty bed
Gathering the pieces
Of the pictures she tore up

A single flower
Both black and white
That doesn't know how to bloom
Without growing thorns

A poet lamenting
Over his many heartbreaks
Without which he wouldn't have
Anything to write about

A horse galloping
Away from a prairie fire
That was started by one
Who wanted to be set ablaze

A newborn child
Without a voice
Without a breath
Only his parents' cries

A dancer in a red dress
a rose in her hand
Plucking away at the petals
For every day confined to a bed

A guitar, broken by one
Whose serenades
Didn't subdue any hearts
But shattered his

A waterfall behind which
No one ever comes to hide
For their blood would be seen
In the clear waters

A fawn, separated from its mother
Who will never escape
The loud sound of silver
Stealing beauty from the world

A crow mourning its fallen friend
Its black feathers scattered
By one who sees them
As a bad omen

A night and a day
A tear and a smile
A birth and a death
I've seen it all

For I am God."

BIRTH OF THE ALMIGHTY

Singing the carol
The one from the land
Of endless winters

Trusting the thought
That the mighty one
Will come

Despite the cold
Through the wilderness
And hostility around
He will rise

Bringing the fire
Salvation in a spark
To change everything

Through the peace
Of the mother
And the bewilderment
Of the father

Birth will come
From blessed, thin air
To bring the light back
To the realm of sin

For the unholy ones
Not to burn
But to see the way
The only truth

Bare and exposed
Loving and absolute
The gateway
To the kingdom

For the lost and weary
Roaming around
This cursed land

Hope will come
With the Spirit
Flowing through him

The young cries will echo
Right to the fallen kings
And the martyrs that we hold
In remembrance

All saints, the ones
Who'll accept him
As their savior
Promised, eternity
From his word only

The enemy, led to the defeat
That he made his home
He never rises
He only lurks

Strength through the revelations
Away from the chaos brewing
In the impure hearts

Not a lake of fire
But a sky of peaceful blue
Where the ones who fear God
Will find their home
When the time comes

Some will be chosen
To spread the gospel
To show glimpses
Of the love that defeats
Everything that poisons the stream

With the translucent waters of faith
Enveloping the drowning many
To carry them back to shore

Where life is green and brown
And is being gently carried
By the breeze
Made of his breath

No fights, only resistance
For the mind not to be infected
The law of man is deceitful
It needs to be dissolved

Agitation and lies
Making the ground shake
His feet will rest on it
To push it back down

We are all blessed
Despite us being forgetful
His beauty prevails
Along with grace

We are saved

THE WORD, IN THE LORD'S BIRD

The Lord says

"Look at the bird
Listen to him
In his feathered innocence

What you think
Is only his soft chirping
Is a message
Of reassurance

You know the tongue
I gave you the gift
Put it in practice

Hold your finger out
There's no reason
For either of you
To fear the other

Let him rest on it
Stand still
And wait for the words
You didn't think
Could be understood

What is he saying?
Is he mentioning
What you always saw
In his colors?

Tell me what you hear"

I listen
And I do hear the words
From this small bird

"The blue you can see on me
Is made of the skies
Beyond which the Lord is found

If you look up
As you walk the gray streets
You'll always see me

I'll be flying around
To share your joy when it comes
Or to lead you back to the right path
When you lose your way

It's upwards, towards God
As he makes the sun shine
It's softly through the clouds
Before the thin waterfalls

Bring nothing but yourself
To every walk of life
His grace is more than enough
For you

I'll keep singing
When you need guidance
But remember
That he's the one
You should always seek

I'm not one of the angels
Though I still have wings
It's a gift, and I'm grateful
So should you be

You've been chosen
You hear his voice
Through me

Now close your eyes
And bathe in the Spirit
Let yourself go
In holiness"

ESCAPING THE DEVIL'S TAVERN

I put the cards on the table
But they all have
A single hole in them

The lady beside me
Tells me that I forgot
To pick up all the shelves
That fell out of my gun

I look down but can't find them
"Search your wounds," she says
I do, and all my clothes
Turn bright red

I should be terrified
But I don't feel anything
We're all numb here
The smoke and drinks help

I stand up, walk around
Trying to find a face
Whose eyes move around
With a semblance of life

But no one seems
To really exist here
It's a secluded place
Where the sun never rises

Endless stairs and rooms
All leading to depraved ways
Of trying to find out
If one is still breathing

Nothing surprises me anymore
The glasses are always full
So that the mist never dissipates
What more could we ask for?

I stumble around and almost fall
I don't think that anyone
Had ever tried to stay standing
For so long in this place

I must sit down
I feel sick, this isn't usual
At least not in body
Only in mind

Have the toxins taken their toll?
I thought that the deal
Was endless liquid bliss
In exchange for our souls

I get frantic, I need some air
And that's when I see it
That shed snakeskin
In front of the door
To the forbidden room

The voice that told us
That we're free to destroy ourselves
In this here nocturnal den
Was very clear
We can't enter this room

But the sight of these aged scales
Is too intriguing for me to resist
I open the door
And enter

It's pitch black, if only for
This lingering red hue
And this horrible feeling
That all good things in the world
Have been violently murdered

I finally see it
The snake, so brown
Crawling around this throne
Slowly revealed by the crimson light

And when it finally shines more brightly
The apparition that ensues
Almost kills me from within

The long black cloak
The red eyes
The perverse smile
This is the worst place
I could have walked into

He says

"I'd told all of you
Not to come here
This is where I retreat
To think about ways
To turn you into ashes

The temptation seems
To have been so strong in you
That you even dared braving
The warning of the one
Who birthed temptation itself

I'm surprised that you're awake enough
To have even left your table
And that you haven't crumbled
At the mere sight of me

But don't be reassured
No one is supposed to see me
You're all meant to be slowly burning
Until the real fire comes

You've all been bitten
By my reptilian messenger
Been given sin as a fountain
To drink from until you drown

But you're still breathing
You're still living
You have no right
Seeing me

It's too late now
I can't take any risks
With any stray lamb
That I'm leading to slaughter
I'll devour you now"

The snake jumps at me
I close my eyes
But nothing happens

I open them again
It stopped right before
It got to my face
Its fangs are so close to me

I see that a white light
Is emanating from me
Making him stand up
From his throne

Now is my time
I open the door
As he runs to me
With a blade in hand

I fall right outside
In an open prairie
Panting, crying

Where has the tavern gone?
It was meant to be
Impossible to leave

I sit up against the trunk
Of an upright willow tree
I see the same light
I saw before

A man, wearing only a gown
Of the purest white
Is standing in front of me

He reaches his hand out
I grab it without hesitation
He tells me to follow him

And I do

CONQUERING HELL ON WHITE, WILD HORSES

There are shadows
Around us
Are they ours?

What if it is the devil
Stuck to our feet
At all times?

I let myself fall
Right into my shadow
To see what's left
On the other side

It's crimson, it's burning
Screams, constant death
I'm petrified by evil
I don't know what to do

The damned souls see me
In their ghostly horror
They jump on me
This is it, I'm gone

I tried to play with the enemy
Mortal that I am
And got tricked into
Giving up on the kingdom

I close my eyes
As it happens
I'm waiting for everything
To collapse into endless torture

But it doesn't
I don't feel anything unholy
I open my eyes

The souls have kneeled
They're looking down
I see a blue light
Emanating from me

The devil appears
And screams

"Why did you bring him
To my realm?
I've already been cast away
His light is blinding

Go away, or you'll make
Everything melt
More than it already has

I tempt the souls
In your mortal world
That's where he interferes
He doesn't touch me

I have my own kingdom
Away from him
This putrid place
He sent me to

Leave this place
With your holiness
Who even are you
To come here
And channel it?"

My Lord and savior
Puts his hand on my shoulder
Lets the Spirit wash over me
The words flow

"Satan, you are defeated
And I came here today
To remind you of that

Every time you close your eyes
You will have this vision of Christ almighty
Endlessly destroying your godless ways

I've cast many of your demons away
By using his holy name
There's nothing
That you can do about it

I've been given the ministry
Like many others
We're spreading the Lord's light
You will go blind

Now, in his name
I cast even more fear upon you
Stay away from my world
Unless you want to be destroyed
For good

There will be a time
Where every soul
Roaming around my world
Will be saved

You had your grip on it
The snake found its way
Into our hearts

But you are no more
The times, they're ending
The righteous will inherit the kingdom

You think that you own the sinners?
Wait until we come down here
On white, wild horses
And save them too

What will you do then?"

SALVATION UNDER NORTHERN LIGHTS

I long for a sky
Made of multicolored lights
And for a cold that doesn't
Seep into my bones

Beaches of black sand
Ever-moving clouds
Calm gray over my head
To make my mind
Feel understood

Some silence at last
Water surrounding me
The moon dictating
Its every ripple

Frozen fields and wilting trees
That never seem
To finally fall to the ground

I want to walk until my feet hurt
I want to breathe an air devoid
Of any ill whispers

I want to see volcanoes
Erupt gently
I want the fire to be
The only thing that I see

Make it the brightest candle
That I've ever seen
I'll roam around it
Hoping to become a firefly

Show me a forest
On top of a mountain
Above the ocean

I'll try to draw it
On a ground that's meant
To be constantly erased
By the thin, white rain

Lead me to a chapel
That stands so shy
In the middle
Of a forgotten meadow

Let the doors open
By themselves, as I get there
Let me be alone in it
Except for one

A young woman, at the front
Praying to the Lord
To show her a way out
Of this island that raised her to be
So tired of it

I'll sit on the same bench
I'll keep my distance
I'll bow my head

I'm not one to look
For stained glass windows
Or to confess to men
Dressed in black

But her and I serve the same God
We only use different words
And a wall of shame constantly stands
Between her and him

She'll open her eyes
And tell me that she's never
Seen me before

That she's met everyone
Who walks or breathe
On this drifting, lonely rock

I'll tell her that I'd grown weary
Of how similar and slow
The seasons are
Where I live

That I'm looking for apparitions
To write and sing about
Under this prism for mirages
That they call their night sky

She'll tell me that God
Never seems to talk to her
And that she feels
So alone

I'll sit closer to her
Put my hand on her shoulder
She'll grab it instead
And hold it tightly

I'll wipe the delicate tears
Rolling down her pale face
She'll ask me
What she's doing wrong

I'll tell her that she's been misled
By the solemn beauty
Of this place that she calls church

That the angels and saints
Aren't to be prayed to
That there's nothing else
To be sacrificed

That there's no need for her
To bruise her knees
As she surrenders
To a man-made altar

That the savior
Is waiting for her outside
In the wide, open spaces
Of this land of hers
That she rejects

I'll tell her to trust me
We'll stand up and walk
To a now pitch white desert

There he'll stand
In all his glory
And the kindest of smiles

His arms will be wide open
She'll gasp and run straight to him
She'll be enveloped by his light

I'll go sit on the edge of the cliff
They'll have a lot of things
To tell each other about

She'll come to me
Sit by my side
Our fingers
Will intertwine once more

She'll tell me
That he's now in her
And that she has
All the time in the world
To get to know him more

In the meantime
She'll rest her head
Against my shoulder

DON'T LET ME DIE ON THIS MOUNTAIN

Father,

I have left a dead soil
That's only soothed
By the most loving balm
And now find myself a stranger
In this land of mine

I'd never seen the lake
Nor felt this crisp, silent air
But the noise of the street
Has remained the same

I have followed you
Back into the night
For the sake of a miracle, the shape
Of a white-winged woman

I have left her behind
So that our embrace
May be swallowed
By a golden light
When she breaks my fall

How fitting, the sight of this mountain
That you've sent me to
When you know that I've always
Feared the lies of the depths

Do believe that I'll climb it
To this desert of white
Where I've long wanted
To sign your name in the snow

Where uncovering any of my fingers
May lead me to never
Playing a single song again

My Lord, give me chants to follow
Let an avalanche fall upon me
For me to get closer to you
If only for a moment

Let the dogs come for me
Before the wolves become enamored
With the scent of the dried poison
That used to make my eyes dim
And claim me back as one of theirs

I'll find refuge in a monastery
Where I'll be told
About the pain of the savior
As if I'm supposed to be the one
Who's still feeling it

Let then a prophecy be etched in my skin
For the misled to see
That the clear waters all around
Needn't be red anymore

I'll say:

"My dear brethren,
Why do you forsake yourselves so?
No thorns are to be worn
Let your flesh be immaculate

Do not let the pigments of stained glass
Be where you see our Lord's beauty
For nothing that is man-made
Shall even come close
To be a painting of the heavenly places

Those wooden crosses around your necks
Which you carry like burdens
Are only good for the fire
That can be alight inside you
If only you surrendered

Step outside with me
As the blizzard tries to claim
Whomever is already dead within
And let go of this shame."

We'll leave the sanctuary
Be bruised, cut, and battered
By all the flying, frozen daggers
And cry

They'll see your face
Its grace and kindness
Fully, for the first time
I'll be gone

Only to be found
In the arms of my beloved
To whom I'll say:

"My sweet,

How I've missed you
In this place where
Air becomes scarce

This rose around your finger
Which bloomed with my devotion
Could have never grown
So close to the skies

The only birds whose tunes I heard
Were merely flying by
Showing me on which side
Of the mountain to fall
And it led back to you

Now let us turn this tiny flower
Into an entire garden
And let a piece of heaven
Take it captive

With its endless warmth
We'll be able to go
As high or low
As God wants us."

GATHER THEM ALL FOR SALVATION

"Gather all of those
Who roam around
Looking for purpose

Walking through deserts
Crawling through mines
Swimming through waterfalls

As they crave some warmth
As they long for shelter
As they whisper in their sleep

About lost lovers
About abandoned dreams
About missing children

Let them come and see
All of those who don't
Trust their senses anymore

Worn out, made weary
By the death and sin
That they see all around

The dust in their shoes
The pain in their hearts
The voices in their heads

Victims of war and treason
Left on the side of the tracks
As empty trains pass by

Hear their hollow voices
As they struggle to put
The heaviness into words

Welcome them to the meadows
For them to see that there is still
Color and life to marvel at

Let them sit down and rest
Their hands and feet, calloused
By their years of senseless labor

As they start to ask
Why they were called upon
And rumblings arise

Let him come, the one
Who answers all prayers
And changes lives

Watch him, as he walks
So lightly, almost floating
Straight down from the mountain

Where he was talking
To the highest one
Who sent him to us

As he walks through the crowd
They slowly turn silent
His presence brings peace

See him as he stands
In front of the congregation
With only a smile and open arms

He utters the words
'My friends, you are loved
By your father, your maker

This world has only fallen
For you to be reminded
Of where your home truly is

All of you are so tired
That you don't see any sense
In waking up anymore

Know that death
Has been defeated
In my name

Let me get closer to you
The lame, the sick, the blind
I will heal you

Let me baptize you
With holy water
You'll be anew

I'll make the holy Spirit
Ignite within you all
You'll finally be awoken

You'll feel this desire
To bring even more of those
Who share your vanquished pain

Let me in, my beloved
Open the door to me
As friends, we'll share a meal
Such is my promise'

Without a sound
Everyone in the crowd
Lifts their hands up

Jesus Christ looks at the skies
They part, and the whitest light
Comes down upon them

They are healed
They are saved
They are free"

I'M GETTING MARRIED

This won't be one
Dripping with metaphors
Or trying to lie
In an impressionist bed

It will be me using
The simplest words
To describe this light
At which I finally decided
To directly look

I'm getting married
Only now do I realize
That it's going to happen

I've wanted it for so long
That it doesn't feel real
Now that it's here

So many heartbreaks
So many drunken nights
So many long, empty looks
At my own eyes in tired mirrors

Telling others, and myself
That I've given up
That I'm happy
With being some lonely tree

I'll tell you, if I'm a tree
Then chop me down
Set me ablaze, and let me be
The fire by which
She drinks her tea

Here I was, thinking
That my fingers were too thin
To prevent a ring from slipping
And falling between the stones

Those that I used to sit on
Watching the ocean crash
Wishing upon a bigger wave
To take my breath away

For me to drift along
Painting the seaweed
And the curious fish
All shades of burgundy

That's her favorite color
But I won't bestow it upon the sun
The entire world would look like wine
It wouldn't be special to her, anymore

We met, I spoke
I laughed, she didn't
She'd been hurt by someone
Who looked a lot like me

She hurt me too
Maybe she wanted us to have
Something in common

I went to sleep
Forever, or so I wished
And even prayed for

But God woke me up
To a loving letter
That could never be burned

She was sorry, she meant it
She'd finally seen
The scared romantic in me

We walked among her friends
The trees, flowers, and bushes
I asked her how she would love
If she allowed herself
To spell that word

She told me that she'll let
Her quiet disposition
Do the talking, embracing, and kissing
And that I should learn a few things
From her affection towards silence

But she loves my words
She can't deny it
Not anymore

They make her giggle
They make her cry
And everything in between

What choice did I have
But to make one
Of her beloved roses
Blossom on her finger?

It took a while, and many tears
As well as a sunny,
Quiet Sunday afternoon

She was still in her sleeping gown
I was in what used to be
The suit that I wore
To my own funeral

I'm full of life, now
I even smile, sometimes
How can I not?
I love her so much

It's so simple, it's so soft
She looks even more pure
Than her wedding dress

What did I say about metaphors?

Anyway,
I'm getting married.

www.ingramcontent.com/pod-product-compliance
Lightning Source LLC
Chambersburg PA
CBHW072345100426
42738CB00049B/1880